Sales is NOT a Dirty Word

The Definitive Guide for Success in Sales

STEVE HEROUX

JONES MEDIA PUBLISHING

Selling is not something you do **TO** someone, it's something you do **FOR** someone.

For Mom and Dad, who always worked as hard
as they could to provide a better life for me.
Thanks for everything and I love you!

CONTENTS

HAVE YOU EVER asked yourself, "Is sales really for me?" We've all done that at some point in our lives if we're being honest with one another. The sales industry is its own unique world, and the majority of salespeople would agree it's almost sadomasochistic. Who else would put themselves through so much physical and mental anguish on a daily basis! The funny part about succeeding in sales is once you reach a certain level of confidence and competence, a career in sales is absolutely the best thing you could ever experience. The toughest part is getting yourself to that point, and most people give up before making it to the mountain top.

The best analogy I can give you when it comes to preparing for a career in sales is as follows:

It would be like someone saying they are going to climb Mount Everest. They know the enormous financial cost, they're aware of the extreme risks, they know the likelihood of failure, and they know there's a chance they may die. Yet, they show up to base camp with some gloves, a sweater, sneakers, and a baseball cap. These people are completely unprepared and have no chance of success. It's exactly the same in sales. Most people show up to appointments without any professional sales skills and think they're going to make six figures in month one. Ummmm, hello, McFly...

Life (or sales for that matter) doesn't work like that! If you want to achieve greatness, you have to be prepared. You've got to put in the time, effort, blood, sweat and tears to *deserve* success in sales.

The reason the median income for a salesperson is about $50K per year is quite obvious. Plain and simple, it's a lack of sales skills. There are many other reasons why most people don't have success, but that's first and foremost on the list. Let's discuss two other prominent career choices which require a significant amount of preparation.

The median annual income for an attorney is about $115K and the median annual income for a physician is about $190K. Why do they earn between two and four times what the average salesperson earns? There are two clear factors that explain how and why. First, they invest in their craft substantially. For attorneys, the average cost to become an attorney is approximately $200K. To become a doctor, it's about $400K. That's without interest by the way!

The second important factor is studying. It takes about seven years to become a practicing attorney (four years undergrad and three years of law school). It takes eight to twelve years, depending on the field of study, to become a physician. Conversely, the average salesperson invests less than $500 a year on their craft. You heard me. They invest less than *$500 a year* on improving their sales skills and ability to sell! The average salesperson doesn't see value in investing their dollars on sales training courses, personal development seminars or sales coaching. They'd rather spend almost double that, roughly $1,000 a year, on Starbucks (this is a remarkably sad but true statistic).

Let me make this crystal clear for you. If you do not invest in your sales skills you will never become a top performer in sales. You may do okay, but you will never truly succeed, and you most certainly will not reach your full potential. What do you think happens to athletes, singers, dancers, mechanics or any other vocation who don't practice their skills and invest in getting better? I think you know the answer.

Invest the time NOW to become proficient, knowledgeable, skilled, and confident in sales, and you'll spend the rest of your life benefitting from it.

SALES IS NOT a dirty word. It really isn't. Society has made it seem so because of everything we've read, heard, and seen since we've been little kids. Salespeople have always been portrayed as slick, slimy, aggressive, and dishonest. In reality, the percentage of salespeople who exhibit these traits is very small. They do exist, and there are many people I've met in this industry I wouldn't want to be within ten square miles of, but most salespeople are good, honest folks who are just trying to make a living. The problem for all of us, unfortunately, is perception. The perception of the proverbial "used-car salesman" will never go away. It's very difficult to break free from a stereotype that's been perpetuated for decades.

In 1975, a movie came out which changed the way hundreds of millions of people lived their lives. Can you guess what movie it was? I'll give you a hint. It involves a quaint little island that suddenly gets terrorized by a 30-foot Great White...

Jaws! To set the record straight, *Jaws* isn't a documentary. It's not an episode on *Shark Week*. It's fiction. In recorded history, there has never been a 30-foot Great White ever captured on film. Yet, people believed these man-eating giants existed a few feet offshore in the waters near their homes. For years, millions of people stopped going in the water. In Indiana! Why?

Perception. One fictional movie based on one fictional book instilled fear in the hearts of many. The odds of you getting killed by a shark are 1 in 264 million. The odds of you getting struck by lightning are 1 in 700,000. The odds of you getting killed in a car crash are about 1 in 100. You all still get in your car every day and don't think twice, right? If you let fear win you'll never lead the life you could live.

Let me put this in perspective for you to show how many people live their lives in fear. Sharks kill about six human beings per year. Human beings kill about 100 million sharks per year. Read that again just to let it sink in. Our fear of sharks, which is baseless and factually incorrect, causes us to kill five to ten percent of the planet's shark population each year. You cannot continue to live your life in fear, as it will not only hold you back, but keep you from doing the things you want to do because you think something bad is going to happen.

I wrote this book because I want you to know there are plenty of salespeople out there who are very successful by doing things the right way. You'll learn that honesty, integrity, and humility are essential traits of the top five percenters in sales, and if you share those same values and moral fiber, you'll soon be joining them at the top of your industry. My online sales course, *Six-Figure Sales Accelerator* (www. sixfiguresalesaccelerator.com) may also be something you enjoy. You'll discover better ways to set appointments, conduct sales presentations, become a more dynamic public speaker, generate tons of referrals, and much more. You'll develop the mindset of a champion that will not only allow your confidence in sales to grow, but also create a high level of success for years to come. You'll get to emulate and duplicate the strategies, processes, and success of hundreds of six and seven-figure salespeople who are having great success in the marketplace today.

This is not a book filled with old-school jargon, regurgitated sales processes from the 70s, or antiquated manipulation techniques. This is a book that's loaded with real-life examples, ideas, and habits, that top performers in sales are using every day to have success in their fields. All you have to do is take what they are already doing and mold that idea or action into your own words, phrases, and ideology. You don't have to re-invent the wheel when it comes to sales. Do what other successful salespeople are doing, put your own twist on it, and you'll have the same success they are having. On to Chapter One!

CHAPTER 1

What I Learned About Commitment from Abraham Lincoln

WHENEVER I HEAR the word commitment, I think about Abraham Lincoln. Lincoln was one of the most successful, beloved, and impactful presidents this country has ever seen. Well before he enacted the Emancipation Proclamation, recited the Gettysburg Address, and ended the Civil War, Lincoln was considered by most people to be a complete failure. Before Lincoln ever attempted to become president, he lived a difficult and challenged life, to put it politely.

He lost his first job at age 22. At age 25, he started a store with a business partner. That partner ended up dying shortly thereafter and Abe lost the business and everything he'd invested with it. Not long after that he lost the love of his life, Ann Rutledge. He then decided to jump into politics as he felt he could have a greater impact on the world in this manner. Abe didn't quite have the rise to success as he hoped he would. He proceeded to lose eight elections during this time! Granted, he did have some wins mixed in between the losses, but before he ultimately became our sixteenth president of the United

States at age 51, Lincoln had faced enough adversity and hardship to fill the lives of ten men.

Every time I think about committing, or why people don't follow through on their commitment, I think of Abraham Lincoln. When I was 25, I decided to make a career change and enter the world of insurance and voluntary benefits. I'd already had great success over the past seven years with Cutco Cutlery. I took quite the leap of faith, as insurance and kitchen knives aren't exactly similar industries and products. I left a great income and opportunity to pursue a new goal, but it wasn't an easy decision. I decided the company with the duck on TV, Aflac, would be my next move. I was so excited to get started once I heard what Aflac could do to protect people and their families in their time of illness or injury. I had this sense I was going to do extremely well with Aflac. I was dead wrong. I failed. A lot. Miserably. Over and over. For four months straight. To this day, I still can't believe I didn't quit.

When I started with Aflac I was about to turn 26, was living with my parents (i.e. the Costanzas for you *Seinfeld* fans), and I had about $600 left to my name. I really needed this to work or I was going to end up *being* George Costanza. My first week in Aflac yielded amazing results. I set fourteen appointments my first day in the field, the most of anyone in our training class, and I was stoked. I proceeded to make zero sales from all those appointments. After seeing my disappointment and lack of results over the first two months in the business, my manager promised me I'd make five grand in December (my third month), and I sorely needed the cash. I ended up making a whopping $25 that month, only $4,975 less than the five grand I was "promised." Ugh.

In my fourth month, which at this point I'm now really hurting for cash and wanting so badly to get the hell out of my parents' house, I finally got my first client. I ended up writing quite a few policies and made about $3,000 in commissions. When I got my check in the mail a few weeks later, I was beyond excited to finally see my hard work had paid off. I opened the envelope with excitement, which then led to concern. There was a weird symbol in front of the dollar sign on the check, which I thought was a hyphen (it looked like this):

-$3,147

So, I asked my manager what that meant, and she said it was called a chargeback. I asked her, "What's a chargeback?" She told me a chargeback is when a client doesn't pay the invoice for the employees' payroll deductions for insurance, and Aflac takes back all the commission they paid you. Ugh, again. My very first client, which I was so excited about, turned out to be a crook. He embezzled all the employees' payroll deductions he was supposed to send to Aflac and then disappeared. To put a cherry on top, he also stole all their health insurance premiums and was never to be seen again. Great start to my new career huh!

The reason I share that with you is because in my first four months in Aflac I had practically nothing to show for it. Zero accounts, less than $500 earned, and an overwhelming amount of disappointment and failure. I worked my ass off for those four months and gave it everything I had. But then, something strange happened. All my hard work finally started paying off! My commitment to working hard every day, no matter what the outcome, finally became worth it. I started getting new accounts, writing a ton of policies, and helping lots of people. My first full year in Aflac (2004), I set the rookie record for sales in New England at that point in time. I won two incentive trips, made some good money, and saved up enough to move out!

My point is this: No matter what your situation or what your circumstances may be, you've got to be committed to success regardless of how long it takes. For me, it took several months of self-doubt, mental anguish, getting yelled at by my parents, having zero cash, and getting told NO a thousand times. For Abraham Lincoln, it took 29 years. Twenty-nine, long, hard years before he reached his ultimate goal of becoming president. So, no matter where you are right now in your life, whether it's your first day in sales or your five thousandth day, you can become successful. You've got to make the commitment to yourself that you're willing to pay the price to reach your ultimate goals in life.

"Don't give up. Don't ever give up." - Jim Valvano

HAVING THE **WANT** TO GET BETTER

Nobody is ever going to be more responsible for your success than you are. As the great Jim Rohn once said, "You've got to practice being like a child." And what's the one thing that comes to mind when talking about having the *want* to get better? Well, let's go back to when you were a kid. Think about your attitude when you really wanted something - a new bike, video game, doll house, ice skates, etc. You were relentless with your parents and wouldn't stop until you got what you wanted. You wanted that item more than life itself and were willing to do anything to get it. Chores, cleaning up your room, no allowance for a year...You we're going to sacrifice it all for that one item. That's how you must be in sales. You must want to be successful more than anything in life. If you do, you'll find a way to make it happen. You'll read more, you'll invest in training courses, you'll attend seminars, you'll seek out mentors, you'll hire a coach - you'll do whatever is necessary to have success in sales. I ask you bluntly, at this moment in time as you're reading this book, do you honestly have the *want* to be a top performer in sales? If so, read on.

UNWAVERING BELIEF IN YOURSELF.

It begins and ends with belief in yourself. If you don't believe you can achieve something, you have no shot. Relying on luck, hopes, prayers, wishes, and whatever other Magic 8-Ball way of thinking you choose to adopt, will end up in frustration and mediocrity. We are all conditioned to "believe" we can or can't do things. According to John Maxwell, by the time we reach the age of 17, we've heard the word NO, 150,000 times. Conversely, also by age 17, we've heard the word YES, only 5,000 times. So, when you've been barraged with negativity from an early age to the tune of thirty times more than the positive, it's no surprise people have a self-confidence problem.

Let me share a story with you about how elephants are trained. You may have heard this before, but it bears repeating. These majestic and powerful beasts are somehow controlled by these tiny, little human beings. With one swipe of its trunk or one step forward, these elephants can crush you in a nanosecond. Obviously, controlling these massive creatures is of the utmost importance and means the difference between life and death.

From an early age, in order to establish control, elephants' legs are tied to thick, wooden stakes, deep in the ground. When they're young, the rope used is very thick so there's no chance they can escape. As they get older they become so used to the feeling of that rope tied around their leg and the feelings associated with it (being stuck and trapped), they never even bother trying to move. A full-grown elephant weighs about 12,000 pounds. A stake in the ground made of rope and wood has literally no chance of preventing an elephant from moving. If that's true, then why don't they just walk normally and pull that stake right out of the ground? The reason? Belief. Their minds have been conditioned, for years since they were an infant, to believe they can't move that stake. Their minds are now trained to not even try or attempt to break free because when they were infants they tried and they couldn't move.

Have you ever seen those videos where elephants are running amuck through towns or have broken out of the circus? Do you know what you're really seeing? An elephant that finally believed in itself.

NO EXCUSES

The reason most people are where they are in life is because of the person in the mirror. It's not the fault of the economy, where they grew up, their parents, their boss, the traffic, the weather, or any other lame excuse. We live in a society riddled with blame, and it's reached beyond epidemic-level proportions. Unfortunately, it's what people see in daily life that gives them this impression. Look at sports for example. When a referee makes a bad call the team that loses always blames it on that one bad call. They don't blame their own inadequacies or their own mental and physical mistakes they made earlier in the game. They blame one little moment, as if that was solely responsible for the loss of the game. It almost never is, Saints fans.

If you're unhappy with your physical condition right now, you have only one person to blame: you. You know exactly what you're supposed to do (and not do) in terms of eating better and making the right food choices. You know you're supposed to work out and be more active. Some of you belong to a gym you pay for every month, yet you don't set foot in there, as if there was an asbestos warning. You know you're overweight and you continue to blame outside factors like your kids, you get home too late, it's cold in the morning, the gym is too packed with people, and every other BS excuse you can think of. When are you finally going to man-up (or woman-up) and take control of your health? Doesn't your family deserve to have you around? Don't you deserve to live a healthy life and live as long as possible? We all have excuses as to why we're not where we want to be in life and as soon as you realize the person who's most responsible is the one reading this book, your life will change almost instantly.

STOP PROCRASTINATING

I don't care who you are, you procrastinate. We all do. If you say you don't, you're lying. JFK procrastinated, Mother Theresa procrastinated, Dr. Martin Luther King procrastinated. You'll never be able to eliminate procrastination because it's nearly impossible to do so. About the best you can do is mitigating and minimizing the time you do it. I love Simon Sinek and pretty much everything he has to say, do, or write. He posted something on Instagram a few months ago and it truly made me respect him even more. The post said, "Just procrastinating." That's why he's awesome! Sometimes it's ok to procrastinate. Yes, I said it. At certain times, procrastination allows you to clear your head, get in a better space, de-stress, and refocus. However, this can certainly be dangerous if you let it go on too long.

Mel Robbins has a great tool to help people minimize their procrastination. She recommends the 5-4-3-2-1 Rule. All that means is when you're avoiding doing a task or project, you just count down backward from five to one and take action! I've used this several times, and I assure you, it works. So, the next time you're procrastinating from doing laundry, cleaning the garage, making cold calls, or loading your CRM, use the 5-4-3-2-1 Rule and watch what happens.

No Giving Up! No Matter What

You've heard this a million times, and you'll probably hear it a million more. There's a big difference between giving up and being savvy when it comes to making decisions. There are some scenarios which require you discontinue an activity because it's no longer providing value to your life or business. I won't pretend I know the answers as to when you should stop these activities, but they occur in all aspects of our businesses, lives, sports, etc. When it relates to life or death situations, there's never, ever, a reason to give up. Someone facing a major illness like cancer or someone facing paralysis and is told they'll never walk again, should never give up. You've got to fight, fight, and keep fighting until the end. I'd rather die than give up, and that's the attitude you must have in sales if you want to be a top-five percenter. You've got to exhaust your last ounce of energy, your last gasp of breath, before you give up.

There's no better example of somebody not giving up than Aron Ralston. You may not remember his name, but Aron Ralston is the guy who was trapped by an 800-pound boulder and had to cut his own arm off to survive. He was hiking alone in a remote canyon in southern Utah when a boulder fell on his arm. The immovable boulder pinned his arm to the canyon wall. After being trapped for five-and-a-half days, he decided he had only one option if he wanted to survive. For 127 hours, he was trapped. His one and only option if he wanted to survive was to cut off his own arm. The problem with that premise was the fact he had only a very dull pocket knife. I cannot imagine the anguish and fear he had to go through mentally to make this life-saving decision. Let alone deciding he had to break his own arm first, before starting to cut. Just thinking about the level of mental toughness and physical pain he must have endured makes me woozy.

Every time I think of a situation that provides me the option of quitting and giving up, I think of Aron. This is the type of mental toughness you need to display if you want to reach the top of your industry in sales. Don't give up because you had a bad start to your career. Don't give up because your parents told you that you wouldn't make it in sales. Don't give up because your boss or manager doesn't believe in you. Have faith in yourself. Be relentless in learning the proper sales skills, developing a bullet proof mindset and commit to being successful no matter what.

CHAPTER 2

Closed Minds Don't Close Sales

"*HAVE AN OPEN mind." "Become more open-minded."*
We've heard these phrases countless times in our lives, haven't we? What do they mean? Having an open mind can mean many things. If you keep hearing this from people they might be trying to tell you something! Typically, when people are told to have an open mind it's because the mind they currently have appears to be closed. It's the stubborn, the egotistical, the omniscient, the know-it-alls, the self-righteous, and the "high IQ" people that seem to lack the open-mindedness that others are seeking or recommending they display.

Open minds have been responsible for ending wars, engaging in space travel, discovering new worlds, and creating artistic masterpieces. It seems to me the close-minded people are the ones who start the wars, destroy relationships, create conflict, and stifle innovation. The human mind is the single, greatest source of gifts we can give to this world. Why would you not use it for the right reasons?

I have a great example of how having an open mind changed my life. I must admit, it's probably one of the first times I used my mind from the "open" perspective. I used to be very closed-minded and truly believed it was my way or the highway. Growing up as a child, I was extremely shy, nervous, and introverted. I did have a few close friends, but I would always shy away from talking to kids I didn't know. From second grade through high school, I barely said a word. I didn't go to any dances. I didn't go to any parties. I didn't have any dates, and I most certainly didn't go to any proms. I just kept my head down in homeroom, didn't talk to anyone and kept to myself. Then, came freshman year of college.

I went to a rather expensive business school outside of Boston, and I was in such fear of the unknown and meeting all these new people. After getting somewhat settled into my school routine, I realized I had to get a part-time job. I knew my parents were paying a ton of dough for my education and I didn't want to have to keep asking them for money. I decided I needed to pull my own weight and help. Just about a week later, I walked into class and saw these little square fliers all over the desks. They looked like this:

$10/appointment!

Customer Service and Sales!

781-XXX-XXXX

I had no idea what the job was, but I decided to call the number and find out. I was deathly afraid of people, and in no way would I ever do a sales job, but I figured it couldn't hurt to ask what the job entailed. I called the number and they asked if I'd like to come in for an interview. I then replied, "So, what's the job?" They said, "It's customer service and sales." I said, "Soooooo, would I have to talk to people or...?" I was hoping for some kind of desk job or mindless data entry-type of position. They then replied, "Yes, you do have to talk to people, but you'll find out how it all works when you get here." For some reason, I decided to go and find out.

Fast forward two hours later and I'm walking out of there with an official offer letter! Well, at least what I thought an official offer letter would look like. The main guy signed it with his expensive-looking pen, so it must be legit. I had no idea at the time, but they hired anyone who had a pulse and was breathing, but they made it seem so exclusive! I went home that night and told my parents I got the job. They said, "Stevie, that's great! What's the job?" I then told them, "Mom, Dad, I'm going to be selling knives." You know that sound of deafening silence? That's what I heard. Nothing.

My dad chimes in and says, "Stevie, you're not doing that. Are you crazy?" I said, "Why not? They're really good knives!" He said to me, "First of all, you barely talk. Second, nobody's going to buy your knives. Third, I'm not giving you the money for the knife kit." In order to get started, you needed to buy this demo set of knives and it was about $130 if I'm remembering correctly. If you know anything about Cutco Knives, paying $130 for $400 worth of knives was a screaming deal back then!

Since my dad shot me down without blinking an eye (he's close-minded when it comes to sales by the way), I turned to my mom and said, "Ma, can I borrow $130?" Of course, Mom said yes, and I got started the following week. I was so incredibly nervous. You have no idea. I had no real business attire, so I had to borrow my dad's ugly brown dress pants and hideous brown tie to go with the only white shirt I had. I looked like a 60-year-old brush salesman from 1955.

On the first day of training, there were about fifty other people in the room when I arrived, so I took my usual spot in the very back of the room, as far away from the front as possible. This ended up proving pointless, as I found out we would have to role-play the scripts out loud with a partner! UGH!! I thought I could hide way in the back and avoid as much human interaction as possible. I barely liked talking to the few close friends I had, let alone role playing a sales script in front of complete strangers. As you can imagine, if training in a hotel meeting room was this scary for me, how the hell would I be able to do this in real life with real customers? I seriously considered not going back for the second day of training, but something inside me told me to stick with it and deal with my fear head on.

To make a long story short, my first three weeks in the knife business went better than I expected. I ended up the #1 college student Cutco sales rep in all of New England! I made $1,600 (which may have well been $16M to a broke college kid) and was beyond excited to show that check to my parents. When I got home I told them I had a surprise. I took out the check, and before I revealed it said to my dad, "You were right, Dad, the knife thing didn't work." He then replied, "I told you it wouldn't work." I replied with a wry smile, "Ha. I'm just kidding, Dad. It worked pretty damn good." I then proceeded to slide the check for $1,600 in front of him. He grabbed it, put his glasses on, looked up and said, "This is from the knives?" I said, "Yep. I told you!"

He looked down, then looked at my mom and said, "Let me see these f**king knives." No joke, he really did say that. Sorry, we're from Boston, it's just how we talk. But he did say it with a smile...

So, I got the knife kit out of the car so he could try them, and I let him use one of the table knives. He then said, "Holy s**t. These are pretty f**king good! Maybe we'll buy some of these." If I could impress my dad with something I was selling, which nobody in the world could ever seem to do, I knew I was on the right path.

Believe it or not, three years later, I went on to become the number one college student Cutco rep in the United States in the second semester of my senior year. I stayed with Cutco for about six years, until age 24, and had great success running sales teams for them. The reason I share this story with you is because I was the *last person ever*, you'd think would be good at sales. If I didn't have an open mind and I wasn't willing to take a huge risk to do something I was deathly afraid of, I wouldn't be where I am today. My entire life, my sales career, and my future were created with that one decision I made to pick up that phone and call the number on that flier in 1996.

BE WILLING TO LISTEN

Your effectiveness in sales is ultimately tied to how well you listen. People ask me all the time, "What's the secret to selling?" There are no secrets, of course, but the closest thing to that "secret sauce" for success in sales is your ability to listen effectively to others. You've got to actively listen to your prospects and customers and truly hear what they are saying. They'll tell you everything you need to know about them, what they're looking for, and how to solve their problems. All you have to do is listen! I can't remember exactly where I found these guidelines on effective listening (I think it was Jeremy Minor), but I absolutely love them and follow these to a T. If you want to become a wonderful listener and see a major improvement in your sales results, follow these guidelines by asking yourself these five questions:

Are you doing something else while the person is talking?

Or are you thinking about your next meeting, event, etc.?

During your conversation with somebody, do you wait for them to pause so you can say something or do you tend to interrupt them?

Are you an interrupter? Nobody likes them.

Are you pretending to listen so you can squeeze in your own comments?

Are you a one-upper? Nobody likes them either.

CLOSED MINDS DON'T CLOSE SALES

Are you aware of the message the person is sending, not only through words, but body language, facial expressions, eye contact, and voice inflection?

Do you pay attention to non-verbal clues like body language and eye contact?

Do you listen through filters?

Do you listen effectively based on the person you are talking to (race, sex, experience, age, success level) or do you judge them based on these factors?

If any of these five actions seem familiar, you are self-sabotaging your ability to listen to people effectively. This, in turn, substantially limits your ability to be effective in communication, which affects all parts of your life, especially your success in sales.

RETRAINING YOUR MIND

If you only had one car for the rest of your life, would you take care of it differently than you do now? Let's just say it's the car you currently drive. How would you change the way you take care of it? Would you get the oil changed on time? Would you wash and wax it regularly? Would you rotate the tires, change the brake pads, keep the washer fluid full? I assume the answer is yes.

The reason you would change the way you take care of it, is because you know it's the only car you'll ever have, so you'll finally see the value of taking care of it. It's the same with our minds. But for some reason we don't seem to take care of them in that way. Your one mind is the only mind you'll ever have. Don't you think you should keep it in great working order? Wouldn't it make sense to ensure it's in tip-top shape, to make sure it functions and operates at full capacity?

Well, if you agree, why aren't you doing it? Our minds are in our control 100% of the time. What we decide to put in our minds, what we decide to fill them with, is all up to us. Filling your mind with negativity, harmful thoughts, hurtful emotions, and destructive outside factors all leads to a dysfunctional mind. How can two people who grew up right next door to each other in the same neighborhood, with the same absentee parents, with the same limited financial means, end up in two completely different places in life? Their mindset, that's how. One of them decided to retrain their mind while the other did not. One of them decided not to settle for what everybody else in the neighborhood settled for and ultimately decided nothing was going to hold them back in life. The other person made the decision to accept the "reality" of their situation. They relegated themselves to the belief nobody ever gets out of the neighborhood and makes a better life. According to them, the opportunities just aren't presenting themselves. They never got a break like some people did. They don't have the money to make something happen, they never got to go to college, yada, yada, yada.

The day you decide to change the way you think is the day your life will change. The first step to changing the way you think is making the *decision* to change the way you think. The next step is implementing the tools necessary to make that change. It's kind of like your health. There are many reasons people are overweight. Most of the time, it's a reflection of the actions and decisions they make on a daily basis (or don't make). Do most overweight people decide to go to the gym or decide not to go? Do most overweight people decide to eat pizza more often than salads? Do people who are in great physical shape, who are toned, fit, and muscular have to make the same decisions? Of course they do! They decide to go to the gym instead of laying in bed. They decide to eat salads more often than pizza. They decide to make the tough decisions and don't take the easy way out.

Your life is a culmination of your daily decisions, which over time, will add up to the finished product. It's up to you to make those decisions, and when it comes to your mind those decisions are crucial. When you decide to willingly infest your mind with garbage, like the nightly news or with negative thoughts and feelings, what kind of life do you think that will lead to? You've got to honestly figure out what type of life you want to live. Once you decide, it's just a matter of the little, tiny decisions you make every day that will make all the difference in the world for you.

ELIMINATING THE "OLD-SCHOOL", BS TACTICS

Have you ever thought about why so many people have such a horrible perception of salespeople? Take a second right now and think about the words you would use to describe most salespeople. What comes to mind? Pushy, rude, aggressive, arrogant, cocky, greedy, slick...any of these pop into your head? If I asked you to draw me a picture of the proverbial "used-car salesman." What would you draw? I think about a guy with a plaid jacket, gold chain, long and greasy hair, and wearing loafers without socks. There's probably not one single car salesman that looks like that, but that's the perception, and it will never change.

The reason we have this awful perception is because of the way we were taught. The experiences we've all had with bad salespeople are too numerous to mention. It's what we see every day on social media, in the movies, and in our daily lives. When the impression of slimy salespeople keeps on being promoted by the masses, how else are we supposed to think? I almost feel like we're continually being told the world is flat, in a sales sense of course. Until Pythagoras or Galileo, whomever you think made the discovery that the world was round, everyone thought the world was flat. Just like the majority of sales trainers, coaches and "gurus" think sales is just about closing everyone and getting anyone to say yes to whatever you're selling. The world is not flat, and sales is not about closing people. Period.

A majority of the sales trainers you see today, all over social media, are modern-day snake-oil salesmen. Many are crooks, criminals, charlatans, liars, and phonies. And I'm being polite. These are some of the actual words these thieves have used to sell their sales trainings:

"Close anyone, any time."
"Get anyone to say yes."
"10X your sales in six months."
"Get three clients in 30 days!"
"Why aren't you selling 12 homes a month?"
"Your daily closing rate will increase 40-100% in two weeks."
"Our average client makes $395,000 per year."

GMAFB. I mean, seriously, some of these people should be arrested. Oh wait, one of them has been arrested. Don't worry though, it was only for fraud, money laundering and felonious activity that lead to being jailed for two years and a judgement to repay $110M in restitution to the people he robbed. And that's who you want to learn sales from? A convicted felon? There's absolutely no regulation on the baseless, BS claims these people are making, and no repercussions for blatantly lying to the public to fleece them.

Selling dreams has been a long-standing trick of the trade when it comes to sales training, and this current-day group of crooks is no different. Do some people double their sales? Yes. In two weeks? Hell no. Do some people "10X" their income? Yes. If they made $947 last year. IT'S NOT REAL. Imagine you were interviewing financial advisors and one of them promised if you invest your money with him, he'll "10X" it! "Your $50,000 investment with me will easily turn into $500,000 within a year. When would you like to get started?" Ummm, I don't think so. #berniemadoff

Let me explain to you what truly works in sales if you want to have a long, happy, joyful, and successful career.

HONESTY
INTEGRITY
HUMILITY

If you have those three traits, that's a great start. Of course, we need to do a ton more than just that, like following the strategies and ideas of the top five percenters, but you need to have a baseline. If you want to be looked at like every other salesperson in the world and continue to follow and learn from these slime balls teaching you all these BS tactics, then be my guest. Be aggressive, be relentless, "act as if", use the ABC method, take no prisoners, use your "yes ladders" and see how much business comes your way. See how many referrals you get. See how many people reach out to you because someone else told them how amazing you are. "Closers" will always be closing, that's for sure. They'll continue to chase business and prospects for the next thirty years. They'll never build a legacy, a reputation they can be proud of, or an honorable life that anyone would be happy to live.

This is the straight-up truth. If this isn't your philosophy I'd recommend you stop reading this book, give it away, or return it, and go try to manipulate another uneducated customer into buying from you even though they don't want to. Harsh huh? The truth hurts sometimes.

BE WILLING TO COPY THE SUCCESSFUL

This may be my favorite quote of all time, and it's so appropriate for the sales industry:

> "Good artists copy. Great artists steal."
> - Pablo Picasso

This couldn't be truer in life, business, or sales. With one caveat, of course: the person you copy from should be the person you'd like to emulate. They should share the same morals, ideals, philosophy, integrity, and lifestyle. Copying someone because they have more money than you is probably the biggest mistake you can make. The biggest false indicator of success in sales is how much money someone earns. I get it,

CLOSED MINDS DON'T CLOSE SALES

money matters. I'm not stupid. We need money to live, provide for children, have shelter, food and water, etc. But I will share with you a lesson I've learned in life, and you've probably heard it before.

Money can't buy happiness. Never can, never will. I know tons of men and women who have way more money than I do and they're miserable human beings. They can count their millions, but they can't count the number of goals their kids have scored in soccer. They can tell you how many followers they have on Instagram, but they can't tell you the last time they took their wife on a romantic date. They can tell you how many units they sold last month, but they can't tell you how many lives they've impacted for the better.

Have you ever seen a cover band before? They play the same music, sing the same songs, have the same sound, use a similar name, and many of these groups are extremely successful. For example, The Australian Bee Gees are a world-renown cover band of ... you guessed it, The Bee Gees. They've been around for more than 20 years and performed more than 6,000 times in 55 countries. They've got tens of thousands of adoring fans and have generated millions of dollars in revenue. They didn't write ONE, single song. They simply mimicked The Bee Gees' sound, found a lead singer with a falsetto voice, and duplicated what the Hall of Fame band has already done. They didn't reinvent the wheel. They didn't create anything new. They got great at what someone else already did and followed their exact path.

My suggestion is this. Find people to follow whose goal in life isn't to make a million dollars, but to impact a million lives. Find people who care more about changing what's on the inside than changing their $10,000 watches on the outside. Find people who have a following because they deserve it, not because they bought it. There are so many amazing people out there in this world who've had massive success in sales and didn't have to sell their souls to the devil to do it. There are tons of men and women who've impacted countless lives because of the way they act, the way they treat others, and the way the carry themselves. There are a thousand different people trying to "teach" you a thousand different ways to sell. Their foolproof sales systems, their guaranteed results, their "secrets" to success will continue to be peddled by these people for years. Follow someone who doesn't need to film their content while riding in their Rolls Royce. Find someone who doesn't need to show you their strikingly beautiful girlfriend (probably hired), their huge mansion (probably rented), or their private jet (also rented and can't leave the runway). I don't pretend to be perfect and I have a ton of flaws, but I can tell you one thing for sure: I sleep like a baby at night and I'm completely happy with my life because I do things the right way. I've learned from so many wonderful mentors in my life that you do not need to mortgage your integrity in order to have success in sales. There are countless people who've chosen to make an impact first and make money second. That's who I'd have my eye on.

CHAPTER 3

Humility: You Don't Need to Tell People You're Humble

HUMBLE IS NOT a word humble people use to describe themselves. Humble is a word that *others* use to describe the humble. Being humble, in and of itself, defies ego. Humility is born from a disposition of giving, acceptance, modesty, and gratitude. People who live their lives humbly don't want fanfare, don't show off, don't act brash, don't self-promote, and don't toot their own horn. They don't record video content in front of their Bentley, they don't take selfies on their private jet, and they don't make sure you can see their $10,000 watch in their ads.

When I think of a person who embodies humility, I think of someone who puts others' needs first. MLK, Mother Theresa, Gandhi are a few people who fit the bill. I think of someone who will treat everyone with the utmost of respect, whether they're rich or poor, black or white, man or woman, human or animal. There are so many wonderful examples of people showing humility in this world, there are too many to list. We all know the story of Warren Buffet, whose net worth is roughly $80B at the time I'm writing this. He still lives in the home he bought 50 years ago for $31,000. He drives a $40,000

Cadillac to work every day. He doesn't need a 20,000 square-foot palace or $300,000 Lamborghini to show his wealth or stroke his ego.

Another person who exhibits humility on a seemingly ongoing basis is Keanu Reeves. On more than one occasion, Neo has shown his soft heart, and he truly cares about the people who've helped him become successful. It's been reported he's given away points, or back-end shares of his earnings, to crews on his movies. He started a foundation to benefit cancer patients after his sister was diagnosed with cancer. But his most humbling moment came a couple of years ago on a New York City subway car.

Not having any idea he was being filmed, he graciously gave up his seat on a crowded train so an older woman could sit down. The act of giving up your seat to a woman or an elderly person is rarely seen these days, but for someone of his "stature" to not feel he is "too good" or "famous" to give up his seat is a breath of fresh air.

Humility was always something that came somewhat naturally to me, being so quiet and soft-spoken and never really enjoying the spotlight. But when I started to get my first little taste of recognition and praise, staying humble became a challenge for me. Early in my CUTCO days I didn't really like being recognized on stage for my accomplishments. As I became more successful I started to feed off of it, and it became a feeling I desperately wanted more of.

I started to see that as a young, successful, and marginally attractive 19-year-old male, there were certain "perks" that came with being the #1 guy. You can figure out what some of the perks were, but let's just say it was sort of like being a rock star (at least that's what it felt like). Tons of people would seek me out, talk to me after events, ask me out on dates, which as you well know, NEVER happened in high school. I must admit, it was very hard to ignore those perks and stay humble at the same time everyone in the world is telling you how great and amazing you are.

There is, however, a negative side of being super successful, which certainly has its drawbacks. During most of my career in Aflac I was almost always the #1 sales rep in my market and constantly recognized, year after year. It became old-hat to me after a while, and people just accepted I would be #1, and nobody seemed to really care anymore. I remember one time at a banquet for year-end awards I was on stage and the Market Director (the Big Wig) at the time said, "Well, everyone, guess who's #1, again...Steve Heroux, blah, blah, blah." There were two people (out of hundreds) that sincerely clapped for me: my girlfriend and my manager - that's it! That was the exact point in time I realized no matter how successful you become, not everyone will be happy for you. Humility is about staying grounded, care-free, and egoless. Practice staying humble no matter how well you do, how much money you make, how many accolades you get, and you'll live a much more fulfilled and purposeful life. I'm living proof.

REALIZE YOU DON'T KNOW IT ALL

It's hard for some people to admit they don't know everything. Do you know someone like this? I want you to think about the feelings you get when you think about a person who's a "know-it-all." I'm sure you'd agree most people don't view that person as open-minded, easy to talk to, or even knowledgeable! They think they are God's gift to society and never think they're wrong about anything. When you go through life thinking you know everything, you're completely missing the boat as to what life is all about. When it comes to sales, if you think you know everything, allow me to let you in on a little secret: you don't. Every day you could be learning something new about sales. There are countless thoughts, ideas, strategies, and processes you've never heard of.

About a year ago I was on the phone with a friend of mine named Harry, who's been in the mortgage industry successfully for over twenty years. A few minutes into our conversation he said he had to call me back because he had to go do something for someone he didn't get as a client. I asked him what he had to do for his non-client, and I was completely blown away! I had never heard of someone doing something like that before! I asked him how long he's been doing this process with clients he *didn't* get, and he told me about twenty years. I then asked if he'd landed any clients from this strategy and how much income he thinks he's earned because of it. "Of course I have. I'd say a few hundred thousand dollars I wouldn't have made otherwise." Mic drop. That exact moment is when I realized there were so many things I didn't know about sales. I hadn't heard of doing anything like what Harry was doing in my 22 years in the sales industry. It turns out there are things other successful six and seven-figure earners are doing daily I had no idea could be done. That moment was the inspiration for my online sales course, *Six-Figure Sales Accelerator*.

I decided I was going to build an online sales course based not only on my personal knowledge and success over the past two decades, but on the daily activities and strategies that six and seven-figure earners in sales were doing in today's marketplace! I wanted to find out for myself what all these amazing sales professionals around the country were doing that I wasn't. If one little conversation with a friend can open my eyes about what I don't know, what would happen if I asked hundreds of other top-five percenters in sales what they were doing every day to have success?

Most online courses and sales trainers teach you the same old regurgitated garbage they've been teaching for decades. I wanted to do something completely different. I wanted to show salespeople what other leaders in their industry were doing today, to have success, not what may have worked in 1989. So that's exactly what I did. Do you know why we don't use beepers or VCRs anymore? Because they don't work as well as the technology we use today. They're obsolete, just like the sales training that continues to be taught by most of the "gurus" out there.

In the year I spent doing research for the Six-Figure Sales Accelerator Online Course, I learned so many amazing things I could have been doing all these years if I had just known about them. If I had only put my ego aside and didn't think I knew everything already, I may be in a better place today. If this topic and idea of understanding that you don't know everything rings true for you, please take some time and check out the course. The knowledge, strategies, ideas, processes, and beliefs of the top-five percent of sales professionals are laid out for you in detail. All you have to do is copy them.

WILLING TO ADMIT YOUR FAULTS

I get it. This one's hard. Nobody wants to admit they have faults, which is probably why so many people think they know everything. For personal growth to happen, you've got to admit you have shortcomings, challenge areas, and thoughts which could be improved. You've got to believe you can handle your emotions better, you can be more efficient and disciplined, and you can take full responsibility when you make a mistake. If you can start on the path to doing all those things, your life will start changing in the blink of an eye. When you can say to someone, "I was wrong and I'm sorry," you'll open up the doors to an entirely new life where people will respect the heck out of you, whether or not you're in total disagreement with one another.

The great Jim Rohn impacted tens of millions of people in his lifetime, and I'm so sad I never got to meet him before his passing. He made an everlasting impression on me, my career, my life, and the way I think. There are too many quotes and ideologies to share, but one that comes to mind when I think about this topic is:

> "Learn to work harder on yourself than you do
> on your job. If you work hard on your job you
> can make a living, but if you work hard on
> yourself, you'll make a fortune."

Working on ourselves is extremely hard work. That's why most people don't do it. If we don't think there's anything to improve on, and we think we know everything, we won't work on ourselves. That's what's holding many of you back. You don't think you have any faults, you don't think you have anything to improve on, and you don't think you need to improve in many areas of your life. No matter how perfect you think you are, you can always get better. We all can. Whether you like him or not, Tiger Woods works on getting better every day, and he has certainly admitted his faults. He won The Masters in 2019, after self-destructing in his personal life and practically losing his ability to play golf just a few years ago. Oprah Winfrey is another example of someone who works on herself every day. She's one of the most successful people on the planet, and has admitted she still has many faults. Drug addicts, alcoholics, and many other people with personal issues have overcome their addictions, because they've admitted they have faults and they're willing to go through hell to correct them. That's why so many people have been able to stay sober for the rest of their lives, yet millions of people never beat their negative habits and addictions - because the first step in doing so is to admit you have a problem.

My dad is the perfect example. He was an alcoholic throughout my childhood for as long as I could remember. He was a great dad, don't get me wrong, but there were certain things he was missing in my life and certain things he was doing that my mom just couldn't take any more. I'll never forget the day when it all hit rock bottom for him (and us).

I was outside my grandmother's house playing with a remote-control car. I loved that thing! I was speeding it up and down the street, doing jumps off the curbs, just having a blast. My dad came out to see how I was doing, and I decided to be annoying for a minute, like any other twelve year old. I started weaving the car in and round his feet, driving it super-close to him as if I was going to hit him and then veering out of the way at the last second. A minute or two later, after doing that several times, I accidentally ran it straight into his foot. I knew it had to hurt because it was going about 30 mph, and I could hear my dad groan when it hit him. He looked at me, looked down at the car that was flipped over from the impact, then smashed it to pieces with his foot.

I was crushed, much like the car that was now in a thousand pieces. He had been drinking and wasn't in a good mood when he came outside. That incident set him off and drove him right over the edge. I ran inside crying, told Mom what Dad just did, and balled uncontrollably for the next ten minutes. My dad eventually came in and apologized, but I didn't want to hear it. Little did I know that one moment was the last straw for my mom. She told him that if he didn't quit drinking that day, she was packing her things, taking me, and never coming back. My dad finally realized if he didn't admit that he had a problem he would lose his family. There comes a point in time where many people lose everything they have because they can't admit fault. We've all got to admit there are certain things we need to work on, or it can be all gone in an instant.

BE OK WITH FALLING ON YOUR FACE A FEW TIMES

It's ok to fail. It's ok to fail a lot. The hallmark of almost every successful person's journey is that it's highlighted with failures throughout. I could give you a million examples of people failing their way to the top. Thomas Edison, Abraham Lincoln, Michael Jordan, and Oprah Winfrey are just a few of these folks. The list of people who failed before they succeeded is too long to list. The difference between the best and the rest is their willingness to embrace failure, not avoid it. Failing guides you in the right direction and will get you back on the proper path to success. It will show you where you were wavering, teetering, or meandering too far off track, and it will snap you back into reality very quickly. Failure also causes massive personal growth. It shows us we may lack maturity, lack execution, lack discipline, or lack strategy. It forces us to completely rethink our plan and drives us to create a different way to achieve the results we're looking for. Failure is a great thing.

People generally don't respect or admire "Trust-Fund Babies" because most of them didn't do a damn thing to achieve success. They got everything handed to them by Mommy or Daddy and got dealt the best hand in life. It's the people who came from nothing and created greatness whom we embrace and respect most. We're drawn to the people who came from nothing, had to overcome every obstacle imaginable, and went bankrupt more than once, before they made it to the mountain top. Failing, and failing a lot, creates an amazing story for you to share with the world on how you ultimately achieved success in your life. Boring, mundane, and uninteresting are the lives of those who've not experienced failure. The most beautiful views are seen at the end of the paths with the most dangerous turns. It's time to start embracing failure and not avoiding it, as failure is the ultimate ingredient to a successful life in sales.

CHAPTER 4

Your Hall of Fame Trait: Discipline

WHEN I THINK of the word "discipline," I think about the military, people who are in tremendous physical condition, and the drill sergeant from Full Metal Jacket. Sorry, I just do. There are two examples of discipline that pop into my head every time I share my thoughts on the subject. The first is an example from the world of professional golf. Many of you know Phil Mickelson. He has 51 professional wins to his credit, five of those are Major Championships. He's probably one of the top ten golfers of all-time and has amassed a net worth of $300+ million. What sticks out to me is the fact he's extremely disciplined in certain areas, but not in others.

When he practices his putting, he does something quite unique. He has one drill where he putts 100 three-foot putts in a row. If he misses just one putt, no matter if it's #9 or #99, he starts over! He doesn't stop practicing until he makes 100 putts in a row. I have no idea how many times in his life he's had to start over, but I can assure you, practicing a hundred thousand or so three-foot putts will turn you into a terrific putter.

On the flip-side, his lack of discipline off the tee has cost him many tournaments and several major championships over the years. On more than one occasion he's taken unnecessary risks during his rounds that have led to self-destruction on the course. He knows he should hit a four-iron off the tee to play it safe and hit the fairway, but instead he hits the driver. If you don't know golf, that's like trying to get a splinter out of your foot using a machete instead of tweezers. It's the wrong tool for the job, no matter how many times you do it. My point is this: No matter how much you try, nobody is 100% disciplined in every area of their life. If you focus on being disciplined *enough* in most areas of your life and business, you'll be extremely successful.

Quick story for you that brings me back to a place in my career when I was fully disciplined. When I first started with Aflac, I had to make a ton of cold calls. And as we all know, nobody likes cold-calling! Ok, almost everyone I know doesn't like it, feel better? I don't care what other people think, but it's not fun for me. Maybe you do actually like it, but I certainly don't. My friend Dave and I started in Aflac around the same time, and we knew if we wanted to make it we'd have to make a ton of cold calls. So that's what we did. We made 125-150 cold calls, almost every day, for a full year. It was the only way we knew, as we had to get clients somehow.

One day early on in our careers, our Market Director walked into our office around 11:30 a.m. He said, "Hey guys, let's go grab some lunch." We both thought that was odd and then told him, "It's only 11:30, we need to make our calls. We'll go at noon." He looked at us with a puzzled look on his face as if we were crazy to not want to go get lunch with him. In reality, we needed to work! We had bills to pay and were committed to being successful. That's discipline. Not only did we have to focus on making 125 calls every day, we also had to ignore all the distractions, the lunch offers, the early happy hours, all of which we had to say no to. It ended up working out pretty darn well as I was able to accomplish what less than 1% of people have ever accomplished in Aflac and Dave has been one of the most successful leaders in the entire company. Being disciplined works. It's the key to success in sales.

CREATING A DAILY ROUTINE

Let me be blasphemous here for one second. You DO NOT have to schedule every second of every day of every week of every year. Am I being clear? Creating routines that are developed from habits are as individualized as snowflakes. The same daily routine for some people will simply not work for others. It's not all about doing what the "experts" say and do and live the way the "experts" live. It's about finding the right daily routines that give you the most joy, productivity, and confidence.

I ask my clients all the time, "What's your favorite thing to do in the world?" I hear a variety of answers. Some common answers are travel, spending time with my family, golf, fishing (that's mine), surfing, etc. Then I ask people, "When's the last time you did that?" The answers would shock you. "Six months." "Two years." "I can't remember!" Imagine not being able to remember doing the thing you love most in the world. That's utterly frightening. If you want a fulfilling and joyful life, you've got to do what you love to do as much as possible. If not every day, at least every week or every month. If you can't manage to do that activity, do something related to that activity or take steps that will allow you to do that favorite activity more. People always want to know the secret to success in sales. One of the "secrets" is being happy. If you enjoy your life and you're in good spirits all the time, it's much easier to make sales.

HOLDING YOURSELF ACCOUNTABLE

This can certainly be a touchy subject in the field of coaching and mentoring, and I'm going to let you know something that will literally change the trajectory of your sales career. Are you ready? If you don't start holding *yourself* accountable, who are you relying on to do so? You cannot rely on outside sources, entities, or individuals to hold yourself accountable. You, and only you, are solely responsible for your success. If you can't hold yourself accountable to complete the actions and daily tasks necessary for success in your sales career, you're probably in the wrong career. Accountability = self-discipline. If you are not able to discipline yourself you have no chance of maximizing your ability and potential. Many people think coaches are supposed to hold their clients accountable. I completely disagree. If I have to be the one making veiled threats, making clients feel bad for not doing what "they were supposed to do," I'm working with the wrong people.

One tip I learned from one of my mentors a few years ago has made a huge difference in the way I hold myself accountable. Granted, it all goes back to being more disciplined, but here's a strategy I think more people could implement that would make all the difference in the world. When you want to do something you like to do (go fishing, eat ice cream, watch Netflix), you probably just do it. What you should be doing instead is rewarding yourself with one of those activities by completing a task or goal beforehand. For example, if I want to watch Netflix, I have to make sure I do ten prospecting calls. If I want to have ice cream, I work out for an hour before I can have a bowl. Using this strategy gives me incentive to complete the tough tasks and gives me a reason to get them done faster. Now, once I've completed the task, not only have I accomplished a small goal, but I can reward myself for a job well done and allow myself to do that thing I wanted.

ELIMINATE DISTRACTIONS

If we could only eliminate our distractions, what a world we would have at our fingertips! Guess what? We can't eliminate them. We can certainly mitigate or minimize them, but we will never eliminate all our distractions. Whether it's work-related, family-related or life-related, distractions are a part of everyone's day, and the most successful salespeople on the planet have found a way to deal with and overcome them. Distractions are a significant time waster and we all know it. There are many companies that generate billions of dollars (Facebook, Netflix, ESPN) because they know people get distracted easily. Our productivity in sales is rendered useless when we continue to do things like check email and organize papers when we're right in the middle of an important project or deadline.

I have two pieces of advice I'd like to share with you that I know will help you in this area. The first thing you have to do if you want to become more productive and minimize your distractions is to recognize what your distractions are. We may not think returning emails or phone calls are distractions, but that's exactly what they are. The best thing you can do is to put all your notifications on silent (when possible) if you are working on a particular project or task. We all think the next call or email is super important and could land us that big client, when in reality it's probably insignificant and can be handled at a later time. A good way to beat this is to have an auto-reply on your email. It states that you are only checking emails at certain points of the day, and if it's a real emergency they can call your cell. I learned this from Tim Ferris and copied his auto-reply word for word. It works.

The second piece of advice to help you mitigate distractions is to start using the 50-Minute Rule. I learned this strategy from Brendan Burchard. He says if you're going to do any task (send emails, prospect, work out) you should do it for fifty minutes without interruption. Then, take a ten-minute break to refresh and refocus your mind before starting another task. Let's think about prospecting and why most salespeople aren't effective. Very few people in sales enjoy prospecting, and we certainly don't want to do it for eight straight hours. Breaking it up into fifty-minute chunks makes it much more manageable, enjoyable, and doable. There are probably a million more strategies and tips to help you with distractions, but if you start by using one or both of these processes you'll start to see your distractions wane and you'll become more productive almost instantly.

BUILD SUCCESS HABITS

This section could literally make up the entire book with the amount of different success habits we could discuss. For time's sake, and to not overcomplicate things, I'm going to share with you three success habits that have not only helped me, but also the top five percenters in sales seem to practice these as well.

#1: Read

Do you know Warren Buffet spends upwards of five hours per day reading; Mark Cuban spends two to three hours a day reading; Oprah Winfrey is known for her Book Club. There's a reason the most successful salespeople in the world are avid readers. And I'm not talking about reading US Weekly, trashy romance novels, or cheat sheets for your upcoming fantasy football draft. I'm talking about reading biographies of amazing people, reading business-related or instructional books, and even blogs or articles written by your favorite mentors and thought leaders. The average American watches 34 hours of TV per week. 34 hours! The average American also earns roughly $35,000 per year. See the correlation? The leaders in the business world are not wasting endless hours watching Netflix. They are reading. Remember, good stuff in, good stuff out.

#2: Pursue Your OWN Goals and Dreams

Too many people spend their entire lives chasing what others believe to be "success." They spend years chasing the goals and dreams of their parents, spouses, and colleagues. The most successful salespeople in the world know exactly what they're chasing, and they'll stop at nothing to accomplish their goals. They don't care about what their parents think, what their friends think, or what some financial "guru" tells them they should be focusing on. True success comes from achieving what you set out to do and what you've always wanted to accomplish, not what someone else thinks you should be doing.

Passion is most evident when you're chasing after something with everything you have in your soul, relentlessly pursuing your dreams with every fiber of your being. If you're not passionately all-in about a specific goal or dream, the likelihood of you achieving it is slim to none. The most successful salespeople involve other people in their goals and dreams, and it's evident how important they are to that individual. Find something that drives YOU, motivates YOU, and gets YOU up in the morning, and when you do you'll know you're on the right track.

#3: **Associate with the Right People**

I remember as a kid my mom telling me if I kept hanging around those "punks" I was going to end up like them. Looking back on that now, she was totally right. I wasn't hanging around the best kids when I was younger. They were troublemakers, thieves, and bullies and going nowhere in life. Some went to jail, some left town, some are still stuck in my hometown and doing nothing with their lives. Around sixth or seventh grade I decided to take Mom's advice and start hanging around nicer, smarter, more respectful, and more future-driven kids than I used to (mostly the nerds, to be honest). It worked out well for me and I've adopted that philosophy to this day. The great Jim Rohn once said, "You are the average of the top five people you spend the most time with." He couldn't be more right, and his advice is still relevant today.

CHAPTER 5

Integrity is Free to Get, Expensive to Give Away

> The quality of being honest and
> → having strong moral principles
> whole; undivided —

INTEGRITY IS THE one thing that costs you nothing to find, but will cost you everything to lose. For the life of me I still can't figure out why people don't defend their integrity with their lives and just give it away for something stupid. I've seen people lose their integrity to make a sale, to cheat in contests, to look better in their parents' eyes, and much more. Is it really worth it? Honestly? Is it really worth not being able to sleep at night? Is it worth making a sale, knowing you're pulling a fast one on someone?

It's the world we live in, and it will never change. There will always be shysters, scam artists, and immoral salespeople who'll do whatever it takes to get someone to buy from them. People tell me the main reason they hire me is because I have integrity, I always tell the truth, and I'm real. I think that's completely normal, and because so many other sales trainers and coaches do the polar opposite, I'm happy to take their clients. Being honest and upfront with people, no matter the situation, is the only way I know how to live. Telling people they have a piece of spinach in their teeth or letting someone know their fly is down before they go on stage is something we should all be doing. Wouldn't you want to know if a giant piece of spinach from lunch was stuck between your two front teeth? Of course you would.

To give you an example of how staying in integrity shaped my life I'd have to share a chapter in my life that I'm not very proud of, but I'm so thankful I went through. I rarely talk about this period in my life because it's so painful and embarrassing, but I feel it's necessary to drive this point home. A few years back I was invited to a dinner party by a friend of my girlfriend. It was in La Jolla, CA, which is one of the nicest and most affluent areas in the country. After we got there I found out it was a pitch for an MLM company (Multi-level Marketing) and I was pretty pissed. I wanted to leave immediately, but for some reason we decided to stay. Long story short, the idea didn't sound too bad after the pitch and my girlfriend and I ended up joining the company.

After a few months in that business I moved up the ranks pretty quickly. The goal, of course, was to recruit as many people as possible into the company which cost $499 to get in. The pitch was focused on selling people the idea you can make a ton of money in very little time. They show you a compensation plan that looks so much better on paper than it really is, just to get your juices flowing about how big your team will be and how much you'll make off them. They then pretty much force you go to their big quarterly events in giant arenas around the country. And yes, they guilt you into going and you have to pay your way every time, 100% of your own expenses.

After about a year I started questioning what I was doing. I was losing sleep at night and very conflicted internally. I continued to mask the truth by making excuses as for why 99% of people don't make money. I called people lazy, not hard working, not committed, not disciplined, and so many other things. I would embellish how much money I was making and tell people they were crazy if they didn't join the company. That's what I saw the people above me doing and unfortunately, I emulated those actions. My "mentors" in the business would also lie about their level of success and how much money they made, and I believed all of it for some reason. There were dozens of examples I saw which clearly showed a lack of integrity coming from the "leaders," so I justified it and thought it was ok because they were doing it and they were the ones making all the money.

The straw that broke the camel's back came after two years in the business. At one of the national events I was recognized for being one of the *Top 20 in North America* at my position. I was brought on stage in front of thousands of people to be recognized for my team's accomplishments. Unfortunately, I was the ONLY one making any money on the team, and it wasn't very much money at all. You'd think it would be easy to recognize it was all smoke and mirrors, all hype, all just the same old racket that's been pulled on millions of people for decades. But it wasn't. Once you lose one bit of your integrity it's easy to lose the rest. The Kool-Aid tastes pretty good when you're in their grasp, and you don't even realize it's about to kill you. That's what happened to me. I lived my whole life guarding my reputation and always made sure I displayed integrity and in those two years I lost it all.

That very day I was recognized in the Top 20 in North America was the last day I spent in that company. The second I walked off that stage, after being recognized in front of thousands of people, I quit. I walked straight up to my coach (yes, I have a coach), Pamela, who thankfully was the one great thing that came out of this awful experience, and I told her I was quitting on the spot. She was flabbergasted at the thought of me quitting considering how much "success" I was having. But for me, it was an easy decision. I looked up at my team in the stands, who were all cheering and clapping for me, and realized, "Not one of these people is making a dime and they're brainwashed into thinking they're going to be millionaires."

The next day I decided to enter the world of sales training, speaking, and coaching, and I haven't looked back. I am so beyond thankful I realized there is nothing worth losing my integrity for. Not money, not fame, not success, not praise. Nothing. To this day, if any decision I have to make will even remotely cause my integrity to teeter, I don't do it. I promise you, if you are honest, real, and tell the truth in all situations, you'll enjoy a happier and more fulfilling life in sales, and there's no amount of money in the world worth giving that up for.

BE HONEST. NO MATTER WHAT.

Words to live by. "If you always tell the truth, you never have to remember what you said." I don't know who said this, but I live my life by this mantra. To me, it sounds so easy and simple to just be honest and tell people the truth. To many others this seems to be a gray area. People in our society like to justify their lying by using other terms and phrases to soften the blow of their immoral actions and behaviors. Here are a few that you may have heard...

"Alternative facts"
"Slip of the tongue"
"Little white lie"
"Embellishment"
"Truthful hyperbole"

A lie is a lie is a lie. If you're in sales and you can't always tell the truth about what you do or the product/service you sell, you should not be in the business. The perception of salespeople is bad enough as it is, and the reason it's so bad is because so many salespeople have lied about what they're going to provide for their clients.

LIFE ISN'T ALL ABOUT "CLOSING" OR MAKING THE SALE

I know you hear it all the time and all over TV and social media, that you can "make millions" and "close anybody" and "10X your income" and a bunch of other nonsense we've already talked about. If you truly and honestly just care about making money and selling anyone at anytime for any reason, this book probably won't resonate with you. The goal of a true salesperson is to provide enough value for their product or service that their prospect will make a decision to move forward and do business with them. That's it. We already know not everyone is going to buy! Yes, can you believe it? Not everyone is going to buy your product/service, and not everyone should. Once you make peace with the facts about life in sales and that not everyone is going to say yes, you'll be much better off.

I was teaching a sales class last year in San Diego and we were discussing how to engage with your prospects when you first

SALES IS NOT A DIRTY WORD

meet them. Some people call this "building rapport" - and you know what I mean when I use that term. After sharing some ideas on how to better build a connection with a prospect you've just met, someone in the crowd raised their hand and asked if they could share something valuable. Of course I wanted to hear what they had to say, and this is what came next.

"Steve, I wanted to let you know that of all the seminars and classes I've ever been to, this one has been the best. You are honest, relatable, and down-to-earth, and I just wanted to thank you personally in front of everyone. I want to let you all know I attended a seminar last month with one of the famous real estate trainers in San Diego and this is what he said about building rapport. He leaned toward the audience."

"You guys want to be successful in sales? Here's how you do it. Fake sincerity."

I couldn't believe it. I told him there's no way a sales trainer said that. He told me it was absolutely true and this guy has said many other things worse than that. The fact this person has big audiences, charges a few hundred a pop to attend his events, and has thousands of clients, is quite alarming. It is beyond disturbing the masses don't recognize that sales is NOT about manipulation. Sales is NOT about dishonesty. Sales is NOT about "closing" someone. It's so scary to me that people who teach others how to make sales by lying, manipulating, being phony, and acting fake can become millionaire trainers in this industry. It's appalling, despicable, and they should be ashamed of themselves.

How do billionaires sleep at night?

Are You Proud of Yourself? Can You Sleep at Night?

When it comes to making decisions, I've always asked myself this very simple question. Can you honestly rest well at night with the decisions and choices you've made? And if you're in sales, can you honestly sleep at night knowing how you treat your prospects, customers, and colleagues? If you're even questioning your sales methods, ideology, and processes, you're doing this sales thing all wrong. There's a point in sales where you'll get to total nirvana. Most of the top five percenters have already reached this point. They're in a place in their lives where they are proud of themselves for how they live their lives. They're proud of the manner in which they conduct themselves on a daily basis in their businesses. Can you honestly say you're proud of the way you live your life and conduct yourself in your day-to-day sales career? If you can't, something is drastically wrong, and you need to address it before it's too late.

How Much is Your Reputation Worth?

beliefs or opinions that are generally held about someone or something

Well? How much is it really worth?

What would it take for you to be willing to step out of integrity, to completely ignore your morals? How much is it worth to you to screw someone over just to make a sale?

shake out of comfort zone —

For many, it's much less than you think. They'll turn from Dr. Jekyll into Mr. Hyde in the blink of an eye to win a sales contest. They'll switch from truthful to deceptive overnight to qualify for an incentive trip. They'll forego all of their self-respect and dignity to get that year-end bonus. So, I ask you again, what's your reputation worth?

If people defended their reputation and character the way they defend their favorite athlete when someone says something bad about them, we'd be in a much better place. People don't seem to care as much anymore about how they are perceived. Social media has made it simple for us to get a glimpse into someone's character without even knowing them. Perception is reality and in the sales profession that means a lot. Your prospects, clients, and future potential employers are looking. They can find out just about anything they want about you these days with just a few clicks. What kind of perception do you want to have in the marketplace? What do you want people say about you when you're not around? What taste are you leaving in people's mouths after you leave the conversation?

Your reputation will cost you almost nothing to build, yet may cost you everything if you lose it.

Believe I'm crazy - find the truth ~

CHAPTER 6

It Takes More than Hard Work to be Successful

NOT MUCH IN life can be accomplished without hard work. There is no substitute for hard work. However, there is something that needs to be pointed out. Hard work, in and of itself, is not a recipe for success. You've got to do more than just work hard if you want to be successful. I can't chop down a tree with just the ax handle: I need the ax blade attached to the end of it. No matter how hard I work, that tree isn't coming down.

I do believe the first step in becoming successful is hard work. Committing to work your ass off will increase your chances of hitting your goals exponentially. But beyond that, you've got to add a few more things to the pot before you have an amazing meal. All the factors we've discussed previously should be part of your recipe for success.

- ✓ Commitment
- ✓ Open Mind
- ✓ Humility
- ✓ Discipline
- ✓ Integrity

There are too many examples to list of hard working men and women around the world who put in crazy amounts of hours in order to be successful. I don't always agree with or condone the number of crazy hours people put in every week. I am not the guy who believes you need to work 100-hour weeks to become successful. Being a workaholic isn't a good thing, just ask the friends and families of workaholics. Jack Ma, founder of Alibaba, recently endorsed and supported the extreme work culture in China's tech industry, known as 9-9-6. It means you must work 9 a.m. to 9 p.m. for six days a week. This is insane to me. Here's his actual quote:

"The real 996 is not simply overtime work," he said, adding that everyone has the right to choose their own lifestyle but those who work shorter hours "won't taste the happiness and rewards of hard work."

You can certainly taste the happiness and rewards of hard work without working an insane number of hours. Working extremely hard and diligently when you're supposed to be working, now that's the key.

Michael Phelps, who we all know is probably the greatest Olympic athlete of all-time, is a perfect example of someone who worked extremely hard to accomplish his dreams. Phelps has won an astonishingly high number of medals at the Olympic Games. 28 total medals, of which 23 are gold! He won six golds at age 19, and five golds at age 31. His achievements will most likely never be matched, and one can probably say the same about his work ethic. Six days a week, Phelps would be in the pool. Not just in the pool for a little while, but five to six hours a day! That's about fifty miles of swimming per week, every single week, for months at a time. On top of swimming he'd lift weights, do flexibility drills, and constantly keep in top physical condition.

Does he have immense talent for swimming? Yes. Is his body and flexibility unique for his size that gives him an advantage? Yes. But those two things alone do not yield 28 medals. He had to pair hard work with his natural ability in order to achieve his dreams. The scary part about his story is that he's been dealing with depression for years. In October 2014, Phelps sought help after spending five days locked inside his room contemplating suicide. "I knew something had to happen fast," Phelps said. "There has to be another way." Even the most successful people on the planet can overwork themselves into a state of depression. It's not all about work, it's about enjoying a happy and healthy life.

How many talented people do you know that never reached their full potential? Johnny Manziel and Cuba Gooding Jr. are just a few of the people you may know who never really "made it." It wasn't because they had all the talent in the world, because talent alone will not do it for you. Robert De Niro's character in A Bronx Tale, Lorenzo, tells his son, "The saddest thing in life is wasted talent." It's so true. Most of the time these folks had all the talent in the world, yet lacked the accompanying work ethic to go with it.

WORK ETHIC - DEFINED

Work ethic means different things to different people. There really isn't one standard definition that makes sense for everyone. When I think of work ethic, I think of my dad. He used to work two overnight jobs, driving a truck for *The Boston*

Herald and *The Boston Globe* newspapers. He did that so I could go to college and have a better life, and I'm so glad I had a father who showed me the value of hard work. So many people don't have the right examples at home or at work to emulate. One factor I think would be common amongst those who you'd consider having a strong work ethic is the setting of standards. Meaning that you, and only you, should set the highest of standards for yourself. Getting up early, taking care of your mind and body, treating people with respect, working until the work is done, and staying focused are all intricate details that make up work ethic. What standards have you set for yourself? Conversely, what do you allow yourself to get away with? Once you figure those things out, you can then decide if you truly have a work ethic you can be proud of.

INNER MOTIVATION

Another overlooked aspect of hard workers is the ability to motivate oneself internally. We discussed earlier that if someone else needs to hold you accountable, your chances for success in sales are slim to none. It's the same for motivation. If you're relying on other factors to get you "up" and to pump your body full of energy to go out and attack the day, you're in the wrong business.

There are three tips I'd like to share with you that will help increase your inner motivation. Here they are:

#1: **Think about what's positive in your business.**

If you can't believe it, you can't achieve it. "Whether you believe you can do a thing or not, you are right." Henry

Ford (it's attributed to him) said this about a hundred years ago and it still rings true. Things are going to go bad for you sometimes. Things go bad for all of us at one point or another. That's just how life works. How you handle those bad things is what determines your level of success in life, and especially in sales. Do your best to never get too high or too low, no matter what happens. When you're constantly on the emotional roller coaster it's tough to sustain a positive work flow and keep your business on track. So, when things aren't going well and you need to flip the switch, think of all the positive things happening in your business (or even in life) and that will get your brain waves moving in the right direction and get back on course toward a productive day!

#2: **Do something nice for somebody else.**

Doing good deeds gives 95% of people a warm and fuzzy feeling. Both the giver and the receiver benefit, and it just makes everyone's day a little bit better. If you're having some struggles staying motivated in your business, take a break, think about someone who could use your help with something, and go do it. It could be someone for whom you'd like to make a business introduction, it could be donating to a charity you haven't given to in a while, it could even be one of your neighbors who needs some work done around the house and may be unable to physically do it themselves. Remember, staying positive and doing positive things for others is the best medicine for almost any mental ailment we have.

#3: **Have a vision.**

When's the last time you sat down in a quiet room with no distractions and visualized exactly what you want your business to look like? If you can't think of a time you've done that, start doing it after you read this! In fact, I'd recommend you stop reading right now and take five minutes to visualize exactly what you want in your sales career. I'm serious, stop reading...

Having a vision for your future is one of the most important things you can do in life, and when you have clear goals in mind nothing can stop you. Even those times when things aren't going great and you need a little burst of motivation, if you simply close your eyes and see the end goal in mind, you'll forget about your challenges in the short-term, and you'll remember that long-term vision is most important. It will always come back to your "why." How strong is your "why" and how hard are you willing to work to achieve it? When you wake up each day with a purpose and a strong reason why you're doing what you're doing, nothing can stop you! If you'd like to read an amazing book that will help you get a clearer vision of what you want, check out "*Start with Why*" by Simon Sinek. You won't be disappointed.

PRACTICE. WE TALKIN' BOUT PRACTICE!

Those of you who are NBA basketball fans will never forget the Allen Iverson press conference where he talks about practice for an hour! If you haven't seen it, YouTube it. It took place in 2002 and he said the word "practice" 22 times! One of the reporters kept harping on why he wasn't at practice, and it took on a life of its own. All joking aside, practice is critically important and is a crucial component of hard work.

Do professional athletes ever practice? Of course. How much? A lot. Do they watch game film? Hours and hours' worth. Do you watch game film of yourself? I doubt it. If it's good enough for multi-millionaires to do daily, why isn't it good enough for you?

Most salespeople have never seen themselves in action. They've never recorded a sales call, never recorded a presentation, never recorded a speech they gave, never recorded a role play session. Yet, they wonder why they're not having the success in sales they want to have. Don't you think if you knew what you were doing wrong, you could identify it and fix it? Don't you think you could make improvements so you don't repeat the actions causing you to miss sales? Your results would change dramatically, and that's an indisputable fact.

GET *IN* YOUR COMFORT ZONE

This isn't a misprint. I'm being dead serious. There are so many myths about success that have been peddled for decades, and this may be the biggest one that's caused the most damage to salespeople. How many times have you been told you have to "get outside your comfort zone?" A hundred? A thousand? It does sound like it makes sense to think you have to get out of your comfort zone to grow; to be like the butterfly or the lobster or some other animal-related analogy. Let me save you some time. If you are *uncomfortable* selling, you have no chance. If you have a team of salespeople who are *uncomfortable* selling, you won't be leading that team for very long. If you go to a restaurant where the head chef is uncomfortable cooking, how's his food going to taste? How about going to the hospital to have surgery and the surgeon operating on you is uncomfortable performing surgery? Would you be ok with the nurse telling you he's just trying to get out of his comfort zone and trying something new? I didn't think so.

Let me show you how this relates to a critical skill in sales and prospecting. There's a huge reason (among many) most salespeople don't like to prospect. Do you know what that reason is? They're UNCOMFORTABLE doing it! They aren't trained properly, they're anxious, they've never done it before, they aren't skilled in sales, and of course, they're not confident. If you don't have confidence in sales, you will never be a top performer. If sales managers spent more time with their teams and helped them become more comfortable with the process of prospecting, their salespeople would become more confident, and in turn, their results would increase dramatically. But most sales managers keep perpetuating the myth that sales is a "numbers game." Wrong. Sales is a skills same. If you think sales is a numbers game, become a telemarketer. For them, it is a numbers game. Let's just call thousands of people and hope one of these schmucks buys something. Sounds like a great business plan. Telemarketers certainly get high-level sales training and are very highly paid, correct? Oh, they don't? Geez, I wonder why? Why do you think companies make robocalls now? No skill needed and no training required, just keep dialing and hope someone buys...

As a salesperson, would you rather make 100 calls to get two appointments or make twenty calls to get two appointments? Seems easy, right? Apparently not. This is the stuff that not only holds salespeople back, but stunts the growth of entire organizations because their sales managers are teaching their salespeople that sales skills don't matter. Just keep dialing and hoping...

"Even the sun shines on a dog's ass someday."

"Even a blind squirrel finds a nut once in a while."

"Even a broken clock is right twice a day."

All of these are awe-inspiring and critically acclaimed thought processes to encourage your sales team to emulate, right? Keep telling yourself or your team that sales is a numbers game. Good luck.

Charles Barkley has been playing golf for decades, and he is "turrible" at golf. Have you ever seen him swing a golf club? If you haven't, please YouTube it. It's a sight you can't unsee. The best way I can describe it is it looks like a baby giraffe trying to stand up after it's born. My point is this: he's hit hundreds of thousands of golf balls over the past 25 years, and he's never gotten any better. In fact, he's actually worse than he used to be. Can you figure out why that is? Because he has the same terrible swing he's always had. If he keeps swinging terribly and incorrectly, and repeats that a hundred thousand times, what's going to happen? NOTHING. It's exactly the same in sales. If you keep conducting cold calls terribly and incorrectly, over and over again, you won't get appointments. If you keep conducting sales presentations poorly, you won't make sales. Simple. Sales is a skills game, and you have to get good at SELLING if you want to become a top performer. Period.

CHAPTER 7

The One Gear You Don't Want to Miss

THE MINDSET SHIFT. Can you truly change the way you think? The answer is…absolutely! There are so many people in this world who could literally change their life in an instant, if only they changed the way they think. Whenever I think of someone who's had a mindset shift, I think about Ronda Rousey. Unfortunately, her mindset shift went in the wrong direction. If you don't know Ronda Rousey, she was one of the most feared UFC fighters of all time. When she stepped in the ring, it was a guaranteed victory. If you don't know how betting odds work, if you're a 3-to-1 favorite to win a fight, you almost always win. Ronda Rousey was routinely a 10-to-1 favorite. What does that mean? It means her opponents had little to no chance of winning. Unfortunately, her career essentially was ended from one swift kick to the head by Holly Holm. And I don't mean her career ended physically, I mean mentally. One unexpected loss ended her reign at the top of her sport.

Ronda Rousey was unbeatable. She was imposing, intimidating, relentless, strong, and everyone knew she was going to win every fight. Unfortunately for her, it took one brief moment, one lapse of judgement, one undisciplined second, and it was all over. She got knocked out and never recovered. Once people knew the "unbeatable" Ronda Rousey was human, it was just a matter of time before other fighters started believing they could beat her. Just like in Rocky IV when Rocky cut Drago. "He's cut! You hurt him. You see, he's not a machine, he's a man!" Rocky went on to beat the unbeatable Drago and changed history. That's kind of what happened to Ronda Rousey. The UFC world was in total and complete shock that she lost. From that point on, she was a different fighter. It was now affecting her in every subsequent fight because she let it. She used to be "invincible," and she thought and believed she was unbeatable, and now she was beatable because she now believed that.

I think back to a time in my career when a mindset shift was needed, and I always go back to the spring of 2007. I was in my fourth year with Aflac, living in Boston, where I was born and raised, and really enjoying myself and my career. I was making great money, had all my family and friends there, and things were going well. With success comes attention, and by that I mean attention from Aflac leaders all around the country who wanted to recruit me to run sales teams for their organizations. I never thought I would leave Boston. I was already making a healthy six-figure income and my Aflac business was thriving. But one day, on an awards trip in Lake Tahoe, it all changed.

The territory director on the West Coast had been recruiting me for two years. Constantly telling me how great it was in Southern California, how much opportunity was there, and how there were no snowstorms! I would repeatedly let her know I was happy and was never moving. Then one day she said something profound that really hit home for me. I was hanging out with the California crew, in the hot tub of course, and loved the camaraderie and friendship I saw with that team. She said to me, "Steve, why aren't you going to come and join us out here in sunny California?" I told her the same thing I had said to her a dozen times already, "I have a great business going that I've built up for the last four years, why would I want to start all over from scratch?" She then said to me something that really struck a chord. She said, "Well, you already started from scratch once and built up a great business, why can't you do it again?" And for some reason, I thought to myself, "*That actually makes sense. Why not?*" So, I told her I would think about it and let her know. The next day, I asked her if she'd be willing to pay for my move, in its entirety. I'd be living in San Diego in two months if she was willing to do that. It took her about one second to tell me yes, and I was off to San Diego!

To this day I can't believe I made that fateful decision and took that chance, left everything behind, and started from scratch almost 3,000 miles away! It certainly took a serious mindset shift for me to realize I could do anything I want, any time I want, and things would work out. I was dead set on never leaving Boston and never leaving my Aflac business behind, but that's exactly what I did. And if I had never had that mindset shift, I certainly wouldn't be where I am today. In just a few years in San Diego, I blew away the numbers I did with Aflac in Boston. I knew a total of two people in San Diego (my girlfriend at the time and her brother, who lived in San Diego). I built a tremendous business out there and created a life for myself I never imagined I could. It took a ton of hard work, dedication, long hours, tons of personal growth, and discipline. But if it all didn't start with that mindset shift, none of it would have happened. What's your mindset shift moment going to be? What's it going to take for you to make the decision you know you need to make to start living the life you want to live?

ABUNDANCE VS. SCARCITY MINDSET

I learned this from a friend and fellow coach, Jesse Martin, and it's such a great way to approach life. In sales, coming from an abundance mindset will lead you to incredible levels of success. Always expecting good things to happen, coming from a place of positivity, and ignoring the curveballs life throws at you will certainly have an impact on your results in a positive way. Here are a few actions that describe people who live in an **abundance** mindset:

positive energy

- You know what you want and you go after it with intensity.
- You look forward to prospecting and making calls every day.
- You anticipate good things and people telling you YES.
- You are expecting to have success, and it's only a matter of time.
- You talk to tons of people, so you can help impact many lives.

Now, let's discuss what happens when you live in scarcity mindset. You're always expecting bad things to happen, coming from a place of "woe is me," and expecting life to always throw curveballs at you. People who believe in Murphy's Law and that if they didn't have bad luck they wouldn't have any luck at all, are not ever going to be top performers in sales. Here are a few actions that describe people display who live in a **scarcity** mindset:

- You know what you want but you don't go after it.
- Procrastination and call-avoidance is prevalent in your life.
- You anticipate objections and people telling you NO.
- There's always a reason (or six) as to why you haven't made it.
- You avoid prospecting because you have a fear of rejection.

ONE BAD MOMENT...

negative energy

difficulties, mistakes

Another mindset action that keeps salespeople from reaching their full potential is they way they handle adversity. Professionals let the little things bother them for thirty seconds, amateurs let the little things bother them for thirty days, and in some cases, thirty years. Let's use the example of a salesperson who gets a flat tire on the way to their weekly sales meeting on Monday morning.

They show up late, miss the meeting, and get yelled at by the boss. At the end of the day a coworker asks them how their day went, and this is their response:

"I had a horrible day. I got a flat tire on the way to work, missed the meeting, and got yelled at by Bill. It sucked."

Let's fast forward to the end of the week. It's Friday, time for happy hour, and that same person gets invited to go out for drinks after work. At the restaurant, someone asks how their week was. Here's their response:

"I had a horrible week. I got a flat tire on the way to work on Monday, missed the meeting, got yelled at by Bill, and it was all downhill from there. The week sucked."

Now, it's the end of the month and time to go over numbers. After the meeting someone tells that same person they looked "really down" and was wondering why they missed their quota by so much that month. Here's their answer:

"I had a horrible month. I got a flat tire on the way to work a few weeks ago, missed the meeting, got yelled at by Bill, and it was all downhill from there. My month sucked."

I think you're starting to get my point! For that person (and the majority of salespeople), they let one bad moment turn into a bad day, a bad week, a bad month, and even a bad year. It's one *moment*…that's all it is! We all have issues, challenges, obstacles and adversity we must overcome. The way you handle adversity will determine your success in sales. People will tell you NO, people will blow you off, people will say you did a bad job and a million other things that aren't necessarily flattering. It's not always going to be wonderful and perfect, but it can certainly be a hell of a lot better when you learn to control your emotions and just chalk up adversity into bad moments, not bad months.

DAILY AFFIRMATIONS

The first thing I think about when I hear the words daily affirmations, and I may be dating myself, is Stuart Smalley.

"I'm good enough, I'm smart enough, and doggone it, people like me."

If you have no idea what I'm talking about, it's a character played by Al Franken on Saturday Night Live in the '90s. Feel free to check it out on YouTube.

Daily affirmations can make a huge difference in your life and your success in sales. Reason being, a critical component to reaching your full potential is the belief you have in yourself. In life, if you don't believe you're good at something you're probably never going to be good at it. It's the same in sales. If you don't believe you have a quality product or service, if you don't believe you give good sales presentations, if you don't believe you're good at getting referrals, you won't ever master those particular areas. *We are our greatest critic*

If our brains are wired to expect NO, as we've heard that word 150,000 times by age 17, how do we reprogram it to be wired to expect to hear YES? One way we can do so is daily affirmations. It's critical to tell yourself you're a great salesperson, a great public speaker, a great presenter, great at getting referrals, etc. If you hear positive things enough, you'll start believing them. That's the key.

If you want to double-down on increasing your chances for success, think about combining your goals with your daily affirmations. If your goal is to earn $100,000 this year, you should be telling yourself every morning:

"I will earn $100,000 this year."
"I will earn $100,000 this year."
"I will earn $100,000 this year."

Think about Bart Simpson writing twenty times on the chalkboard before class how he's not going to stab Milhouse with pencils any more. Same idea!

What you put in your mind is what you get out, and if you're always telling yourself positive things and stating what you're going to accomplish, maybe you'll start believing it.

CHAPTER 8

Hey! There's Some Water in that Glass!

WE'VE BEEN HEARING for decades that in order to be successful you must have a positive attitude. Well, guess what? It's true! You can't accomplish very much in life when you don't look for the best in life, situations, and people. How many people do you know that are the "Negative Nancy" type? The ones who not only believe in Murphy's Law, but think it was made specifically for their life? The ones who always say, "If it wasn't for bad luck I wouldn't have any luck at all." Or, "This stuff always happens to me. Never fails." Unsurprisingly, these folks are always the ones who complain about their situations, can't seem to get ahead in life, don't have meaningful relationships, and struggle to have the success in sales they feel they deserve.

There was a time in my life when I was just like these people. I always thought negatively, I never got my hopes up, and I didn't have a positive attitude. I used to always think to myself, *"Why does this always happen to me?"* But one day after a conversation with one of my mentors I completely changed the way I think. I started looking for the bright side, intentionally looking for the silver lining, and a very short time later my entire outlook on life changed. More importantly, my sales career skyrocketed. I started enjoying the people I was around and finding the best qualities in each of them. I started viewing my sales career in a different way and stopped worrying about my "lack" of success. I have such a wonderful and recent example that exemplifies why you should always have a positive attitude and make the best of every situation.

If I haven't mentioned it yet, I spend a good amount of time in the beautiful country Costa Rica. My place sits at the top of a mountain, overlooking the jungle and I have about a 180-degree view of the Pacific Ocean. It's serene, tranquil, and relaxing. On my last trip to the States, my plans got slightly derailed, to say the least. I was heading to Ohio and Michigan to see several clients over a five-day period. Of course, I had packed just a carry-on and enough clothes for five days. The plan was to see those clients, then fly back home to Costa Rica before my next trip to the West Coast three weeks later. The trip went tremendously well, my clients were super happy and thankful, and I met some amazing new friends.

I was excited to head home from Detroit, yet nature didn't seem to be as excited as I was to let me leave! Thanks to a snow storm, my flight was delayed and we took off an hour late. The problem with leaving late was that I had very short time window to make my connecting flight in Ft. Lauderdale, and it was going to be cutting it really close with the delay. We landed with about 25 minutes to spare before my next flight, so I ran like Usain Bolt to get to the gate on time. I just made it! As I got to the gate I saw the gate was already closed. They left!! There were eight of us going from Detroit to Costa Rica, and they decided to just sell our seats to the people waiting on standby, ignoring the fact we were just a little bit behind.

I won't mention the name of the airline, but it rhymes with Schpirit.

Long story short, we "missed" our flight and the next flight to Costa Rica wouldn't be until the next day. I decided, in that moment, I would stay in South Florida and catch up with my parents (who live about three hours away). My mom was getting her knee replaced the following week, so I figured I'd surprise them and help Mom out for a little bit. I then decided to call an old Aflac buddy to see if he'd like to have me come and train his team. Since I was already there in South Florida, he agreed to have me come in on short notice. That lead to several new happy clients, and more importantly, new friendships. I then reached out to two more regional managers with Aflac who also were super nice and very interested in what I could do to help their teams. They also agreed to have me in on short notice, and things could not have gone better. After having such great interest in what I do and not enough days to see everyone, I cancelled my second flight back home and decided to spend an extra two weeks in Florida.

On top of that, I reached out to my ex-girlfriend's brother (yes, we're still friends), who also runs a company in South Florida, and asked if I could come and do a training for his sales team. He loved the idea and had me in several days later.

The silver lining is that I got to spend an extra week with my parents when my mom was recovering from her knee surgery, I got to see old friends I hadn't seen in ten years, I reconnected with my former potential brother-in-law and his family, I acquired dozens of new clients, I got to finally go to my favorite artist of all time's museum (Salvador Dali), I visited the best drive-through safari in the U.S., and I lost five pounds! After missing my connecting flight back to Costa Rica I could have been pissed. I could have yelled at the customer service rep like all the other irate passengers did, I could have complained I was losing money because of the cancelled flight(s), and I could have been upset I had to go buy new clothes, as I only had enough for four days! You've got to make the best of every situation no matter what happens, because you can't change it anyway. Always look at the glass half full, find the positives, look for light in dark situations, and I promise you, your life will be much more enjoyable and fulfilling.

ALWAYS LOOK FOR THE GOOD

Wouldn't it be fun if you could only see the good in every situation? I mean really, think about this one for a minute. If all you could see was the good and it was impossible to see anything negative, how would your life change?

You need to think like Shallow Hal. Stay with me on this one. If you haven't seen the movie, it's about a guy who can only see the stunning, outside beauty of a woman. Jack Black plays the character, and no matter whom he looks at, these women are Miss America-like and perfect tens in his mind. In reality, it turns out they are not always perfect tens to everyone else who sees them. Gwyneth Paltrow plays the perfect ten, but in reality, in everyone else's eyes, and even her own eyes, she's not. It's a great movie to show people that there's so much more to life than someone's outer beauty. He ends up falling in love with her in the end because of who she is inside, not because she's a size two.

It's the same in sales. You've always got to look for the good in every situation. When you don't make a sale, is it a bad thing? Of course not. You may have learned something about that particular industry that doesn't jive with your value proposition. You may learn something about the way you presented that you can now change for future sales presentations. You may learn to either say or not say a particular word or phrase. There are tons of things you can learn from failing, and I promise you, you'll learn a hell of a lot more from failing than you'll learn from succeeding.

Be Joyful and Live Happy

Everyone has their own definition of happiness. To some people, it means enjoying what you do for a living. For others, it means having an amazing family and home life. Many people derive happiness from inanimate things like money, cars and other possessions. Others derive happiness from traveling to exotic and far-off locations. Whatever makes *you* happy in your *life* is the only thing that really matters. The definition of happiness is very broad, but there are some habits many of the happiest people in the world all do on a daily basis.

Happiness is a choice, and the folks who tend to be the happiest are the ones who go out every day and try to achieve it. Let's say that gardening really makes you happy. You love being outdoors, taking care of things and taking pride in growing a beautiful garden. You can decide to be in your garden every morning. You can decide to read about new planting techniques and the best fertilizers. You can decide to try growing a new fruit or vegetable, based on what you read on Instagram. Either way, you are *deciding* to do the things that make you happy. All you must do is make the decision to do the things that make you happy, and believe me, you'll be happier!

HAVE AN ATTITUDE OF GRATITUDE

If you study the great ones like Jim Rohn, Simon Sinek, and Zig Ziglar, you'll find they have many traits in common. Hard work, dedication, personal growth, and self-belief are just a few of those traits. There is one specific trait that seems to be overwhelmingly present in the most successful people on the planet: gratitude. Not only do they all teach that *gratitude* is an essential human quality, but they practice it themselves, albeit in different ways, and they make it a point to have an "attitude of gratitude" every day.

I can assume you've heard a thousand times you need to be grateful. You've been told to write thank you notes, reflect about what and whom you are thankful for every day, or even write it all down in a journal. The one thing that matters most is that you practice some form of gratitude *daily*. It's not important what that practice is, but critical you DO the practice *daily*. Even though it doesn't seem as if being grateful will immediately change your life, it's about the feeling you get and the mindset you put yourself in when you have an "attitude of gratitude."

Giving does so much more for the giver than it does for the receiver. Giving thanks and being grateful allows both parties to get a sense of peace, calm, and good will. There is no substitute for thanking someone for doing something nice, and if you don't thank people or let them know you are grateful it can have the opposite effect. Think about the last time you bent over backward for someone and they didn't thank you. How did their reaction (or lack thereof) make you feel? Now, think about the last time someone thanked you for the most insignificant of favors you did for them. How did that make you feel? Quite a difference, isn't it?

Think about some practices you can put into place to start living a life of gratitude. Maybe it's writing down three things you're grateful for each day (I learned that from Brendan Burchard). Maybe it's meditating about whom and what you're thankful for. Maybe it's calling one person every day to thank them for being your friend, colleague, client, etc. Once you adopt an "attitude of gratitude" your results in sales, let alone life, will be completely different.

NICE GUYS FINISH last, right? Does that also mean nice salespeople finish last? NO to both! Over the last ten years, thanks to the meteoric rise of social media and video content, we've been bombarded with so much garbage in relation to having success in sales. The "ABC – Always Be Closing" garbage from 1992's *Glengarry Glen Ross*; the "You can be anyone you want to be on the phone," crap from the movie, *Boiler Room*; and they best one yet, *Wolf of Wall Street*, which has too many cringeworthy lines to mention. When did it become ok to be a lying, conniving, phony, money-laundering crook? When did it become cool to make up fake testimonials from clients, rent mansions and tell people you live in them? Or to perpetuate the myth of getting rich quick over the weekend? Somebody has got to take a stand and call to light this abhorrent and irresponsible behavior.

There are so many great men and women in the field of sales you would be happy to emulate and follow. Countless individuals who do things the right way and make their families proud of them each day. Life isn't all about the money, possessions and fame. The modern-day snake-oil sales trainers will continue to promote that having a Bentley and some gold-digger trophy spouse is some sort of perfect life. It's not. Most of the decent and genuine people in the sales profession don't care about your $300,000 car that has $6,000 oil changes, or your private jet that costs you $1M a year just to maintain. These egomaniacal, self-fulfilling individuals can keep their shiny toys, airbrushed headshots, and spray-tanned trophy wives.

Give me someone who believes in living right, treating people with respect, and giving people an example of how a true sales professional should carry themselves. When I was a kid I wasn't taught money was the be-all end-all to happiness in life. I was taught to work your ass off to provide for yourself and for your family, and if you could lay your head on your pillow at night after an honest day's work, that's what it's all about. Somehow, we've lost that. It's now cool to count how many followers you have, as if that's some sort of prize in the game of life. We've been taught to "ring the bell" and glamorize the fact that you just "closed" someone.

You must always remember: *Sales is NOT a Dirty Word*. A career in sales is something you should be proud of. It's a career that can give you everything you've ever wanted out of life, whatever that may be. As long as you do the right things, you always put the needs and wants of your customers first, and you conduct yourself with honor, integrity, and humility, the sky's the limit for you. When you adopt the mentality of the salesman who can sell anything to anyone, you're going to be in for a long and lonely life. Have you ever heard the phrase, "That guy could sell ice to an Eskimo?" Let me ask you this...

What do you think it says about someone who would sell something to a customer they already have endless amounts of, they can get that said item for free, and they don't really need? When your life is over and people mention your name, what do you want them to be saying? Instead of the dates of your birth and death on your gravestone, what if it listed the amount of lives you've had a positive impact on? How high (or low) would that number be? Sales is something you do FOR someone, not something you do TO someone, and once you understand this critical component to selling, you'll be on the right track to success in sales and you'll enjoy a life you never thought possible.

Acknowledgments

THERE ARE WAY too many people to thank who contributed to my success in some way. Some are very close to me and some I've never met. Some helped provide content for this book and some helped provide content for my life. Here's the list, in no particular order:

Janet and Steve Heroux
Jim Rohn
Simon Sinek
Les Brown
Eric Thomas
Gary V
Jeremy Miner
Jeremy Jones
Pamela Cournoyer
Jesse Martin
Brendan Burchard
Mel Robbins
Keith Ferrazzi
Brian Tracey
Zig Ziglar
Tom Corley
Dan Negroni
Harry Dennis
Brian Traichel

Mark Haber
Micheal Hart
Eric Gillman
Daniel Goleman
Napoleon Hill
Dale Carnegie
Matthew Killingsworth
Daniel T. Gilbert
Mark Manson
Dr. Steve Peters
Dr. Bruce Perry
Forbes Magazine
National Sleep Foundation
Success Magazine
Harvard Business Review
NBC News
CNBC
Big Think
Huffington Post
Buzzfeed
Yourstory
New York Times
Entrepreneur Magazine
Positive Psychology Program
The Quintessential Mind
Psychology Today

QUICK WITTED, HIGHLY engaged and especially authentic, Steve Heroux is a professional sales trainer, keynote speaker, author, and leading authority in providing cutting-edge strategies on selling in today's marketplace. With more than 22 years of success in sales and sales leadership, he has generated tens of millions in sales, helped thousands of salespeople achieve success, and reached the Top 1% of his field in multiple industries.

Steve reached #1 nationwide in new accounts, beating out over 60,000 agents in a Fortune 200 company. He rose to the pinnacle of success in two different industries, product sales and insurance sales, and his clientele include representatives of companies including Aflac, Keller Williams, and the UPS Store, just to name a few.

If you're looking for the same old, regurgitated, and slimy sales training drivel, that's been taught for decades, Steve is most certainly not your guy. Conversely, if you're looking for someone to teach and train you or your team the "right" way to be successful in sales, who is down-to-earth, honest, and will show you the true power that communication combined with integrity can bring you, Steve is your guy.